The Keyboard Family
Takes
Center Stage!

by Trisha Speed Shaskan   illustrated by Robert Meganck

PICTURE WINDOW BOOKS
a capstone imprint

Special thanks to our advisers for their expertise:

Rick Orpen, PhD, Professor of Music, Gustavus Adolphus College
Terry Flaherty, PhD, Professor of English, Minnesota State University, Mankato

Picture Window Books
1710 Roe Crest Drive
North Mankato, MN 56003
www.capstonepub.com

Editor: Jill Kalz
Designer: Lori Bye
Art Director: Nathan Gassman
Production Specialist: Jane Klenk
The illustrations in this book were
created digitally.

Printed in the United States of America in North Mankato, Minnesota.
102013
007757R

All books published by Picture Window Books
are manufactured with paper containing at least
10 percent post-consumer waste.

Library of Congress Cataloging-in-Publication Data
Shaskan, Trisha Speed, 1973-
The keyboard family takes center stage! / by Trisha Speed Shaskan ;
illustrated by Robert Meganck.
p. cm. — (Musical families)
Includes index.
ISBN 978-1-4048-6045-2 (library binding)
1. Keyboard instruments—Juvenile literature. I. Meganck, Robert. II.
Title.
ML549.S47 2011
786'.19—dc22
2010001088

3

We're called keyboards because each of us has a row of keys. In order to play us, musicians press the keys.

Strike!

ANNA, the piano

Here's my dad. He's a harpsichord. My mom's an electric keyboard, and my brother, George, is a pipe organ.

Twang!

DAD, the harpsichord

Each member of my family works in a different way. We make different sounds too. But the way we're played is the same. That's what makes us a family.

MOM, the electric keyboard

GEORGE, the pipe organ

keys

Pianos sound full and rich. When a musician presses one of my black or white keys, a tiny hammer inside me moves. The hammer strikes a string.

Each key is connected to a different hammer and string. And each string makes a different sound.

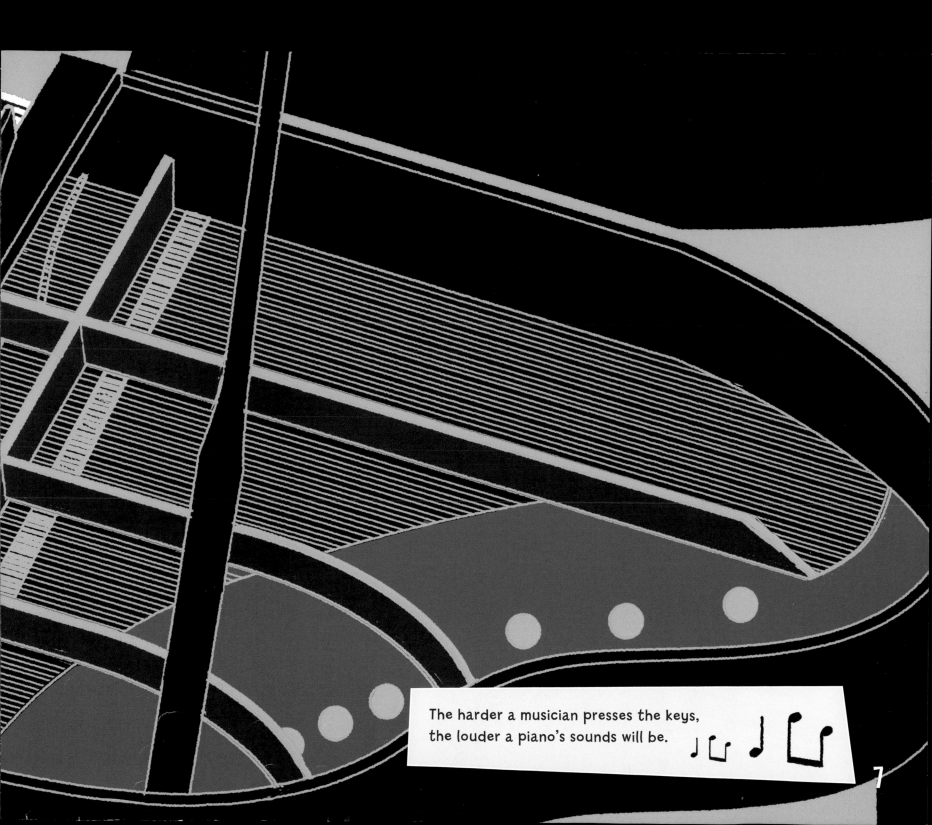

The harder a musician presses the keys, the louder a piano's sounds will be.

7

This is what the movement inside a piano looks like.
The hammers are covered with a soft cloth called felt.

string

hammer

key

8

There are no hammers inside a harpsichord. When a musician presses one of my Dad's keys, a small quill plucks the string. The plucking makes a harpsichord sound thin and bright.

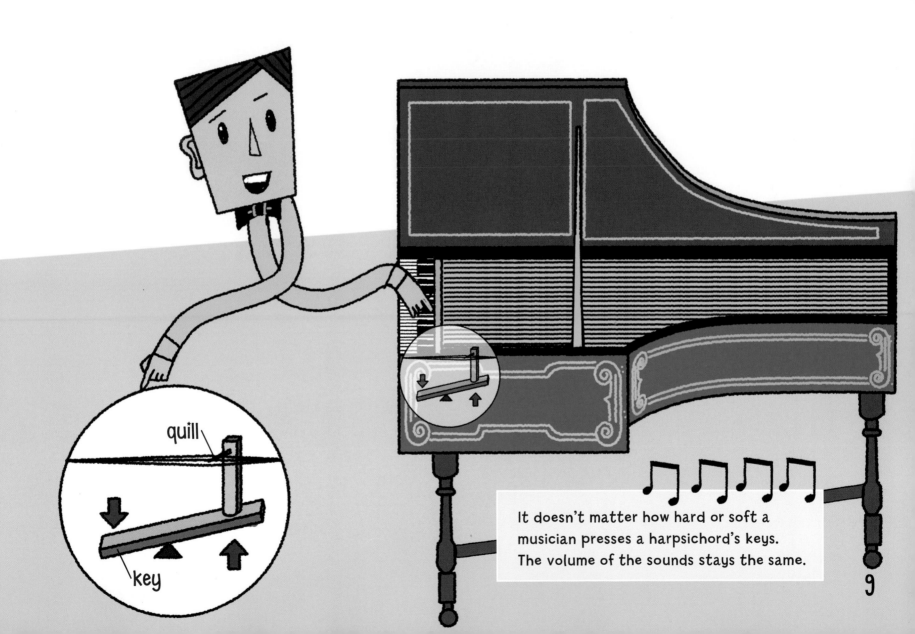

quill

key

It doesn't matter how hard or soft a musician presses a harpsichord's keys. The volume of the sounds stays the same.

9

My brother, George, is a big guy. Like all pipe organs, he sounds very grand. He can play bold, beautiful music in church one day and spooky music in a haunted house the next.

10

When a musician presses an organ key, air is forced through a metal pipe. This air movement creates sound.

DUN, DUN, DUN, DUNNNN!

Organs also have a pedal keyboard, or pedalboard, at their base. The large keys are played with the feet and usually make the lowest sounds.

My mom makes the most awesome sounds ever! Electric keyboards are the only keyboards that need to be plugged in to make music.

When a musician presses an electric keyboard key, a message zips to the keyboard's computer. The computer turns that message into a signal and sends it to the speakers. ZAP! Each signal is a different sound.

Electric keyboards have between 49 and 88 keys. They can include hundreds of built-in drum beats and other instrument sounds. Many have computer displays and can help you compose music.

My family has been practicing for a big talent show. We're each playing our own song, called a solo. But only one instrument will win first prize.

I'm playing a piece by Beethoven.

Ludwig van Beethoven was a German composer and piano player, or pianist.

Dad is playing a piece by Bach. George is playing one too. We fill the house with our music.

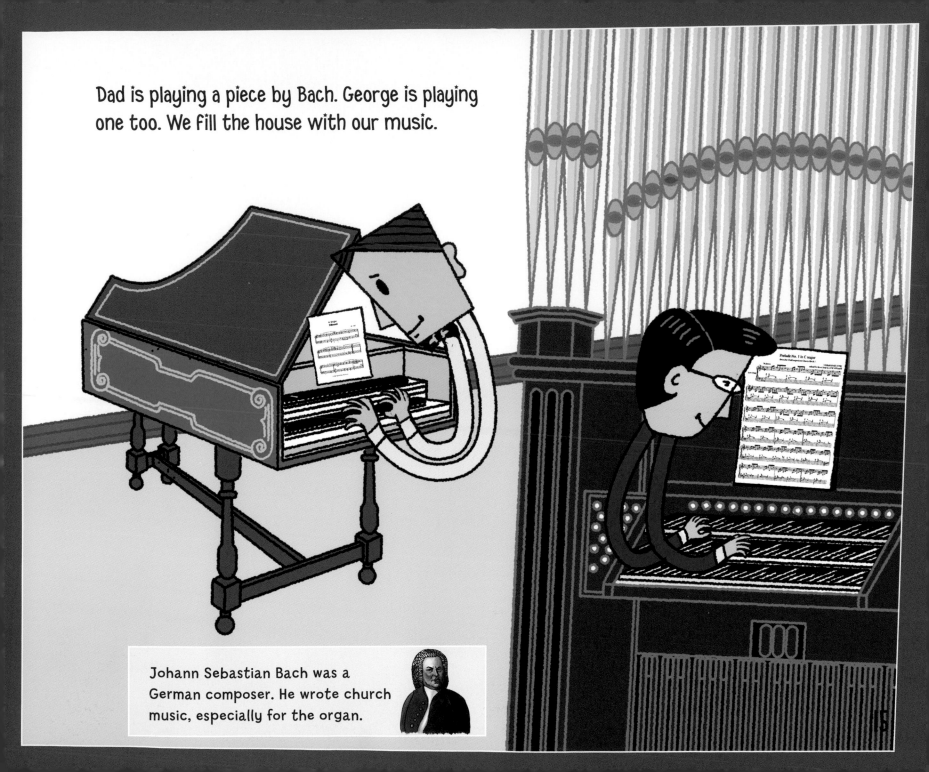

Johann Sebastian Bach was a German composer. He wrote church music, especially for the organ.

Mom picked a song by Ray Charles. Ray Charles played soul music. Soul is a mix of different musical styles, including gospel, rhythm and blues, and jazz. Mom sounds like trumpets and saxophones. She sounds like pianos and drums, long into the night.

Today is the big day! The place is packed! I go first in my family. Beethoven's piece leaps and dances. It rises and falls. When I'm done, the crowd claps and whistles.

18

My dad plays next, then my brother. The crowd stands up and claps for them too.

"Anna, the piano, from the Keyboard family!"

My family cheers. The crowd claps and rises from their seats again.

Glossary

compose—to put together or to write
composer—a person who writes music
musician—a person who plays music
pluck—to pull at and then let go of
quill—a hollow, sharp needle or spine
solo—a piece of music played by just one instrument
volume—how loud or soft a sound is

Fun Facts

The piano was invented in the 1700s by an Italian named Bartolomeo Cristofori.

The harpsichord was invented about 300 years before the piano. At first, it had just one keyboard, or manual. But in the 1600s, craftsmen started building harpsichords with two.

The German composer Johann Sebastian Bach had 20 children. Five of them were named Johann.

The famous composer Wolfgang Amadeus Mozart called the organ the "king of instruments."

Over time, composer Ludwig van Beethoven lost his hearing. But even when he was deaf, he still wrote amazing music. One example is Beethoven's Ninth Symphony.

To Learn More

More Books to Read

Barber, Nicola. *Should I Play the Piano?* Learning Musical Instruments. Chicago: Heinemann Library, 2007.

Helsby, Genevieve, with Marin Alsop. *Those Amazing Musical Instruments.* Naperville, Ill.: Sourcebooks, 2007.

Witmer, Scott. *Drums, Keyboards, and Other Instruments.* Rock Band. Edina, Minn.: ABDO, 2010.

Internet Sites

FactHound offers a safe, fun way to find Internet sites related to this book.
All of the sites on FactHound have been researched by our staff.
Here's all you do:
Visit *www.facthound.com*
FactHound will fetch the best sites for you!

Index

Look for all the books in the Musical Families series:

Around the World with the Percussion Family!
The Brass Family on Parade!
The Keyboard Family Takes Center Stage!
Opening Night with the Woodwind Family!
The String Family in Harmony!